IF FOUND PLEASE RETURN TO:
_____
_____
_____
EMAIL: _____
REWARD: _____

MY WEDDING PLANNER

Wedding Checklist

12 TO 14 MONTHS FROM THE BIG DAY

Determine your budget from the dress to the honeymoon ☐

Pick your Wedding Party ☐

Start making your Guest List ☐

Book Venues and lock in your dates ☐

Book Photographer, Videographer, Florist, Caterer & Band ☐

9 MONTHS FROM THE BIG DAY

Book Entertainment ☐

Decide on Menue and Drinks ☐

Pick Dress - Leave time for 3 appointments for alterations ☐

Gift Registry - Pick 3 retailers to register for ☐

Create Wedding Website ☐

6 MONTHS FROM THE BIG DAY

Order Invitations ☐

Begin planning the Honeymoon ☐

Pick Bridesmaids Dresses ☐

Send Save the Dates ☐

Arrange transportation - Limos, Carriage, etc. ☐

Begin Planning the timeline for your wedding day ☐

wedding Checklist

4 TO 5 MONTHS FROM THE BIG DAY

Book rehersal dinner venue ☐

Check on invitations and make final order ☐

Meet with bakery for Cake tasting and final tasting ☐

Buy shoes and start fittings for gown ☐

Schedule hair and makeup appointments ☐

3 MONTHS FROM THE BIG DAY

Finalize menu and flower selection ☐

Order favors for tables if desired ☐

Schedule second fitting ☐

Finalize ceremony and reception program order ☐

Have menu cards and programs printed ☐

Purchase rings - Giving time for sizing and engravings ☐

2 MONTHS FROM THE BIG DAY

Touch base with all hired professionals ☐

Meet with photographer and finalize videography ☐

Review playlist with band or DJ ☐

Send out invitations ☐

Wedding Checklist

1 MONTH FROM THE BIG DAY

Complete guest list from RSVPs ☐

Get marriage license ☐

Send Rehersal dinner invitations ☐

Schedule final fitting for gown ☐

Send out all final payments to vendors & hired professionals ☐

Confirm hair and makeup appointments ☐

Assign seating ☐

Purchase thank you gifts for bridemaids, groomsmen..etc. ☐

Write vows ☐

1 WEEK FROM THE BIG DAY

Confirm all times with vendors & hired professionals ☐

Send timeline to wedding party ☐

Pickup the dress ☐

Send final guest list to caterer and venues ☐

Pack for the honeymoon ☐

Enjoy your perfect Day!

For better moodboard view this paper is left blank.

Wedding Moodboard

Add your moodboard pictures here.

Wedding Moodboard

Add your moodboard pictures here.

Wedding Moodboard

Add your moodboard pictures here.

Wedding moodboard

Add your moodboard pictures here.

Monthly To Do

Sun	Monday	Tuesday	Wednesday

Thursday	Friday	Saturday

Notes

_____
_____
_____
_____
_____
_____
_____
_____
_____
_____
_____
_____
_____
_____
_____
_____
_____
_____
_____
_____
_____
_____
_____
_____
_____
_____
_____
_____
_____

📅 MON.

_____

_____   ○ _____
_____   ○ _____
_____   ○ _____
_____   ○ _____
_____   ○ _____
_____   ○ _____
_____   ○ _____
_____   ○ _____
_____   ○ _____
_____   ○ _____

📅 TUE.

_____

_____   ○ _____
_____   ○ _____
_____   ○ _____
_____   ○ _____
_____   ○ _____
_____   ○ _____
_____   ○ _____
_____   ○ _____
_____   ○ _____
_____   ○ _____

📅 WED.

_____

_____   ○ _____
_____   ○ _____
_____   ○ _____
_____   ○ _____
_____   ○ _____
_____   ○ _____
_____   ○ _____
_____   ○ _____
_____   ○ _____
_____   ○ _____

THU.

_____
_____
_____
_____
_____
_____
_____
_____
_____
_____

○ _____
○ _____
○ _____
○ _____
○ _____
○ _____
○ _____
○ _____
○ _____
○ _____

FRI.

_____
_____
_____
_____
_____
_____
_____
_____
_____
_____

○ _____
○ _____
○ _____
○ _____
○ _____
○ _____
○ _____
○ _____
○ _____
○ _____

SAT.

_____
_____
_____
_____
_____
_____
_____
_____
_____

SUN.

_____
_____
_____
_____
_____
_____
_____
_____
_____

MON.

_____
_____
_____
_____
_____
_____
_____
_____
_____
_____

○ _____
○ _____
○ _____
○ _____
○ _____
○ _____
○ _____
○ _____
○ _____
○ _____

TUE.

_____
_____
_____
_____
_____
_____
_____
_____
_____
_____

○ _____
○ _____
○ _____
○ _____
○ _____
○ _____
○ _____
○ _____
○ _____
○ _____

WED.

_____
_____
_____
_____
_____
_____
_____
_____
_____
_____

○ _____
○ _____
○ _____
○ _____
○ _____
○ _____
○ _____
○ _____
○ _____
○ _____

THU.

_____

- ○ _____
- ○ _____
- ○ _____
- ○ _____
- ○ _____
- ○ _____
- ○ _____
- ○ _____
- ○ _____
- ○ _____

FRI.

_____

- ○ _____
- ○ _____
- ○ _____
- ○ _____
- ○ _____
- ○ _____
- ○ _____
- ○ _____
- ○ _____
- ○ _____

SAT.

SUN.

MON.

_____

- _____   ○ _____
- _____   ○ _____
- _____   ○ _____
- _____   ○ _____
- _____   ○ _____
- _____   ○ _____
- _____   ○ _____
- _____   ○ _____
- _____   ○ _____
- _____   ○ _____

TUE.

_____

- _____   ○ _____
- _____   ○ _____
- _____   ○ _____
- _____   ○ _____
- _____   ○ _____
- _____   ○ _____
- _____   ○ _____
- _____   ○ _____
- _____   ○ _____
- _____   ○ _____

WED.

_____

- _____   ○ _____
- _____   ○ _____
- _____   ○ _____
- _____   ○ _____
- _____   ○ _____
- _____   ○ _____
- _____   ○ _____
- _____   ○ _____
- _____   ○ _____
- _____   ○ _____

THU.

_____

_____
_____
_____
_____
_____
_____
_____
_____
_____
_____

○ _____
○ _____
○ _____
○ _____
○ _____
○ _____
○ _____
○ _____
○ _____
○ _____

FRI.

_____

_____
_____
_____
_____
_____
_____
_____
_____
_____
_____

○ _____
○ _____
○ _____
○ _____
○ _____
○ _____
○ _____
○ _____
○ _____
○ _____

SAT.

_____
_____
_____
_____
_____
_____
_____
_____
_____
_____

SUN.

_____
_____
_____
_____
_____
_____
_____
_____
_____
_____

MON.

- ○
- ○
- ○
- ○
- ○
- ○
- ○
- ○
- ○
- ○

TUE.

- ○
- ○
- ○
- ○
- ○
- ○
- ○
- ○
- ○
- ○

WED.

- ○
- ○
- ○
- ○
- ○
- ○
- ○
- ○
- ○
- ○

THU.

○
○
○
○
○
○
○
○
○
○

FRI.

○
○
○
○
○
○
○
○
○
○

SAT.

SUN.

📅 MON.

_____

_____   ○ _____
_____   ○ _____
_____   ○ _____
_____   ○ _____
_____   ○ _____
_____   ○ _____
_____   ○ _____
_____   ○ _____
_____   ○ _____
_____   ○ _____

📅 TUE.

_____

_____   ○ _____
_____   ○ _____
_____   ○ _____
_____   ○ _____
_____   ○ _____
_____   ○ _____
_____   ○ _____
_____   ○ _____
_____   ○ _____
_____   ○ _____

📅 WED.

_____

_____   ○ _____
_____   ○ _____
_____   ○ _____
_____   ○ _____
_____   ○ _____
_____   ○ _____
_____   ○ _____
_____   ○ _____
_____   ○ _____
_____   ○ _____

THU.

_____

_____ ○ _____
_____ ○ _____
_____ ○ _____
_____ ○ _____
_____ ○ _____
_____ ○ _____
_____ ○ _____
_____ ○ _____
_____ ○ _____
_____ ○ _____

FRI.

_____

_____ ○ _____
_____ ○ _____
_____ ○ _____
_____ ○ _____
_____ ○ _____
_____ ○ _____
_____ ○ _____
_____ ○ _____
_____ ○ _____
_____ ○ _____

SAT.

_____
_____
_____
_____
_____
_____
_____

SUN.

_____
_____
_____
_____
_____
_____
_____

Additional To Do List

Important Reminders

Wedding Budget

CEREMONY

	Est. Cost	Act. Cost	Deposit	Final Payment
Officiant				
Notice Fees				
Music				
Total				

FLOWERS

	Est. Cost	Act. Cost	Deposit	Final Payment
Bouquets, Corsages				
Ceremony Flowers				
Reception Flowers				
Bouquets, Corsages				
Total				

RECEPTION

	Est. Cost	Act. Cost	Deposit	Final Payment
Venue Hire				
Canapes				
Reception Drinks				
Wedding Meal				
Drink during Meal				
Evening Foods				
Evening Drinks				
Wedding Cake				
Table Decor				
Additional Venue				
Total				

Wedding Budget

ENTERTAINMENT

	Est. Cost	Act. Cost	Deposit	Final Payment
Reception				
Dinner Background				
Evening				
Total				

TRANSPORTATION

	Est. Cost	Act. Cost	Deposit	Final Payment
Bridal Transport				
Groom's Transport				
To Reception				
Additional Bridal				
Guest Transport				
Total				

WEDDING ATTIRE

	Est. Cost	Act. Cost	Deposit	Final Payment
Bride's Dress				
Bride's Accessories				
Bridesmaids Dress				
Bridesmaids Acc.				
Groom's attire				
Groomsmen's attire				
Rings				
Total				

Wedding Budget

HAIR & MAKEUP

	Est. Cost	Act. Cost	Deposit	Final Payment
Bride's Hair				
Bridesmaids Hair				
Mother of the Bride				
Bride's Makeup				
Bridesmaids Makeup				
Mother of the Bride				
Total				

STATIONARY

	Est. Cost	Act. Cost	Deposit	Final Payment
Invitations				
Postage				
RSVPs				
Menus				
Place Cards				
Table Searing Plans				
Table Nymbers				
Thank you Cards				
Total				

Wedding Budget

GIFTS

	Est. Cost	Act. Cost	Deposit	Final Payment
Bridesmaids				
Groom				
Parents				
Ushers				
Flower Girl				
Ring Bearer				
Favors for Guests				
Total				

PROFESSIONALS

	Est. Cost	Act. Cost	Deposit	Final Payment
Photographer				
Videographer				
Wedding Planner				
Wedding Stylist				
Total				

MISCELLANEOUS

	Est. Cost	Act. Cost	Deposit	Final Payment
Accomodations				
Wedding Insurance				
Contingency				
Honeymoon				
Miscellaneous				
Miscellaneous				
Total				

Wedding Budget

OTHER

	Est. Cost	Act. Cost	Deposit	Final Payment
Total				

Wedding Budget

TOTAL

	Est. Cost	Act. Cost	Deposit	Final Payment
Ceremony				
Flowers				
Reception				
Entertainment				
Transportation				
Wedding Attire				
Hair and Makeup				
Stationary				
Professionals				
Gifts				
Miscellaneous				
Other				
Total				

Wedding Vendors

CEREMONY VENUE

Name	
Address	
Phone	
Email	

RECEPTION VENUE

Name	
Address	
Phone	
Email	

OFFICIANT

Name	
Address	
Phone	
Email	

WEDDING PLANNER

Name	
Address	
Phone	
Email	

Wedding Vendors

PHOTOGRAPHER

Name	
Address	
Phone	
Email	

STATIONER

Name	
Address	
Phone	
Email	

VIDEOGRAPHER

Name	
Address	
Phone	
Email	

BAND

Name	
Address	
Phone	
Email	

Wedding Vendors

FLORIST

Name	
Address	
Phone	
Email	

CATERER

Name	
Address	
Phone	
Email	

HOTEL

Name	
Address	
Phone	
Email	

TRANSPORTATION

Name	
Address	
Phone	
Email	

Wedding Vendors

CHOREOGRAPHER

Name	
Address	
Phone	
Email	

DJ

Name	
Address	
Phone	
Email	

MUSICIANS

Name	
Address	
Phone	
Email	

DJ

Name	
Address	
Phone	
Email	

Wedding Vendors

ROLE _____

Name	
Address	
Phone	
Email	

ROLE _____

Name	
Address	
Phone	
Email	

ROLE _____

Name	
Address	
Phone	
Email	

ROLE _____

Name	
Address	
Phone	
Email	

Wedding Vendors

ROLE _____

Name	
Address	
Phone	
Email	

ROLE _____

Name	
Address	
Phone	
Email	

ROLE _____

Name	
Address	
Phone	
Email	

ROLE _____

Name	
Address	
Phone	
Email	

Bridal Shops

Shop Name	
Contact Person	
Style	
Price	
Notes	

Shop Name	
Contact Person	
Style	
Price	
Notes	

Shop Name	
Contact Person	
Style	
Price	
Notes	

Shop Name	
Contact Person	
Style	
Price	
Notes	

The Perfect Dress

BOUTIQUE INFORMATION

Bridal Shop	
Address	
Phone	
Consultant	
Notes	

THE GOWN

Style	
Designer	
Size	
Price	
Date Ordered	
Fitting Date 1	
Fitting Date 2	
Fitting Date 3	

ACCESSORIES

Headpiece	
Garter	
Shoes	
Jewelry	
Other	
Other	

SOMETHING SPECIAL

Something Old	Something Borrowed
Something New	Something Blue

Bridal Party

PARENTS OF THE BRIDE

GRAND PARENTS OF THE BRIDE

MAID OF HONOR

BRIDESMAIDS

Bridal Party

PARENTS OF THE GROOM

GRAND PARENTS OF THE GROOM

BEST MAN

GROOMSMEN

Gift Registery

Registered at	
Registry Name	
Website	
Notes	

Registered at	
Registry Name	
Website	
Notes	

Registered at	
Registry Name	
Website	
Notes	

Registered at	
Registry Name	
Website	
Notes	

Paper Goods Checklist

INVITATIONS & CARDS

Save the Date Cards and Envelopes ☐

Will you be My Bridesmaid, Maid of Honor ☐

Engagement Party Invitations & Envelopes ☐

Rehersal Dinner Invitations & Envelopes ☐

Thank you Cards & Envelopes ☐

WEDDING STATIONARY

Invitations ☐

RSVP Cards ☐

Accomodation & Information Cards ☐

Invitation Envelopes ☐

Envelope Liners ☐

RSVP Envelopes ☐

RECEPTION STATIONARY

Programs ☐

Signage ☐

Table Numbers ☐

Place Cards ☐

Favour Labels ☐

Menue ☐

Registery Wish List

KITCHEN ELECTRICS

KNIVES

COOKWARE

Registery Wish List

BAKEWARE

DINNERWARE

FINE CHINA

Registery Wish List

FLATWARE & SERVING PIECES

GLASSWARE

TABLE LINENS

Registery Wish List

BEDDING

BATH

BARWARE

Registery Wish List

DECOR

OTHER

Notes

Guest List

Name	RSVP	Mailed?	Table#
	☐ Yes ☐ No	☐ Save The Date ☐ Invitation	
	☐ Yes ☐ No	☐ Save The Date ☐ Invitation	
	☐ Yes ☐ No	☐ Save The Date ☐ Invitation	
	☐ Yes ☐ No	☐ Save The Date ☐ Invitation	
	☐ Yes ☐ No	☐ Save The Date ☐ Invitation	
	☐ Yes ☐ No	☐ Save The Date ☐ Invitation	
	☐ Yes ☐ No	☐ Save The Date ☐ Invitation	
	☐ Yes ☐ No	☐ Save The Date ☐ Invitation	
	☐ Yes ☐ No	☐ Save The Date ☐ Invitation	
	☐ Yes ☐ No	☐ Save The Date ☐ Invitation	
	☐ Yes ☐ No	☐ Save The Date ☐ Invitation	
	☐ Yes ☐ No	☐ Save The Date ☐ Invitation	

Guest List

Name	RSVP	Mailed?	Table#
	☐ Yes ☐ No	☐ Save The Date ☐ Invitation	
	☐ Yes ☐ No	☐ Save The Date ☐ Invitation	
	☐ Yes ☐ No	☐ Save The Date ☐ Invitation	
	☐ Yes ☐ No	☐ Save The Date ☐ Invitation	
	☐ Yes ☐ No	☐ Save The Date ☐ Invitation	
	☐ Yes ☐ No	☐ Save The Date ☐ Invitation	
	☐ Yes ☐ No	☐ Save The Date ☐ Invitation	
	☐ Yes ☐ No	☐ Save The Date ☐ Invitation	
	☐ Yes ☐ No	☐ Save The Date ☐ Invitation	
	☐ Yes ☐ No	☐ Save The Date ☐ Invitation	
	☐ Yes ☐ No	☐ Save The Date ☐ Invitation	
	☐ Yes ☐ No	☐ Save The Date ☐ Invitation	

Guest List

Name	RSVP	Mailed?	Table#
	☐ Yes ☐ No	☐ Save The Date ☐ Invitation	
	☐ Yes ☐ No	☐ Save The Date ☐ Invitation	
	☐ Yes ☐ No	☐ Save The Date ☐ Invitation	
	☐ Yes ☐ No	☐ Save The Date ☐ Invitation	
	☐ Yes ☐ No	☐ Save The Date ☐ Invitation	
	☐ Yes ☐ No	☐ Save The Date ☐ Invitation	
	☐ Yes ☐ No	☐ Save The Date ☐ Invitation	
	☐ Yes ☐ No	☐ Save The Date ☐ Invitation	
	☐ Yes ☐ No	☐ Save The Date ☐ Invitation	
	☐ Yes ☐ No	☐ Save The Date ☐ Invitation	
	☐ Yes ☐ No	☐ Save The Date ☐ Invitation	
	☐ Yes ☐ No	☐ Save The Date ☐ Invitation	

Guest List

Name	RSVP	Mailed?	Table#
	☐ Yes ☐ No	☐ Save The Date ☐ Invitation	
	☐ Yes ☐ No	☐ Save The Date ☐ Invitation	
	☐ Yes ☐ No	☐ Save The Date ☐ Invitation	
	☐ Yes ☐ No	☐ Save The Date ☐ Invitation	
	☐ Yes ☐ No	☐ Save The Date ☐ Invitation	
	☐ Yes ☐ No	☐ Save The Date ☐ Invitation	
	☐ Yes ☐ No	☐ Save The Date ☐ Invitation	
	☐ Yes ☐ No	☐ Save The Date ☐ Invitation	
	☐ Yes ☐ No	☐ Save The Date ☐ Invitation	
	☐ Yes ☐ No	☐ Save The Date ☐ Invitation	
	☐ Yes ☐ No	☐ Save The Date ☐ Invitation	
	☐ Yes ☐ No	☐ Save The Date ☐ Invitation	

Guest List

Name	RSVP	Mailed?	Table#
	☐ Yes ☐ No	☐ Save The Date ☐ Invitation	
	☐ Yes ☐ No	☐ Save The Date ☐ Invitation	
	☐ Yes ☐ No	☐ Save The Date ☐ Invitation	
	☐ Yes ☐ No	☐ Save The Date ☐ Invitation	
	☐ Yes ☐ No	☐ Save The Date ☐ Invitation	
	☐ Yes ☐ No	☐ Save The Date ☐ Invitation	
	☐ Yes ☐ No	☐ Save The Date ☐ Invitation	
	☐ Yes ☐ No	☐ Save The Date ☐ Invitation	
	☐ Yes ☐ No	☐ Save The Date ☐ Invitation	
	☐ Yes ☐ No	☐ Save The Date ☐ Invitation	
	☐ Yes ☐ No	☐ Save The Date ☐ Invitation	
	☐ Yes ☐ No	☐ Save The Date ☐ Invitation	

Guest List

Name	RSVP	Mailed?	Table#
	☐ Yes ☐ No	☐ Save The Date ☐ Invitation	
	☐ Yes ☐ No	☐ Save The Date ☐ Invitation	
	☐ Yes ☐ No	☐ Save The Date ☐ Invitation	
	☐ Yes ☐ No	☐ Save The Date ☐ Invitation	
	☐ Yes ☐ No	☐ Save The Date ☐ Invitation	
	☐ Yes ☐ No	☐ Save The Date ☐ Invitation	
	☐ Yes ☐ No	☐ Save The Date ☐ Invitation	
	☐ Yes ☐ No	☐ Save The Date ☐ Invitation	
	☐ Yes ☐ No	☐ Save The Date ☐ Invitation	
	☐ Yes ☐ No	☐ Save The Date ☐ Invitation	
	☐ Yes ☐ No	☐ Save The Date ☐ Invitation	
	☐ Yes ☐ No	☐ Save The Date ☐ Invitation	

Guest List

Name	RSVP	Mailed?	Table#
	☐ Yes ☐ No	☐ Save The Date ☐ Invitation	
	☐ Yes ☐ No	☐ Save The Date ☐ Invitation	
	☐ Yes ☐ No	☐ Save The Date ☐ Invitation	
	☐ Yes ☐ No	☐ Save The Date ☐ Invitation	
	☐ Yes ☐ No	☐ Save The Date ☐ Invitation	
	☐ Yes ☐ No	☐ Save The Date ☐ Invitation	
	☐ Yes ☐ No	☐ Save The Date ☐ Invitation	
	☐ Yes ☐ No	☐ Save The Date ☐ Invitation	
	☐ Yes ☐ No	☐ Save The Date ☐ Invitation	
	☐ Yes ☐ No	☐ Save The Date ☐ Invitation	
	☐ Yes ☐ No	☐ Save The Date ☐ Invitation	
	☐ Yes ☐ No	☐ Save The Date ☐ Invitation	

Guest List

Name	RSVP	Mailed?	Table#
	☐ Yes ☐ No	☐ Save The Date ☐ Invitation	
	☐ Yes ☐ No	☐ Save The Date ☐ Invitation	
	☐ Yes ☐ No	☐ Save The Date ☐ Invitation	
	☐ Yes ☐ No	☐ Save The Date ☐ Invitation	
	☐ Yes ☐ No	☐ Save The Date ☐ Invitation	
	☐ Yes ☐ No	☐ Save The Date ☐ Invitation	
	☐ Yes ☐ No	☐ Save The Date ☐ Invitation	
	☐ Yes ☐ No	☐ Save The Date ☐ Invitation	
	☐ Yes ☐ No	☐ Save The Date ☐ Invitation	
	☐ Yes ☐ No	☐ Save The Date ☐ Invitation	
	☐ Yes ☐ No	☐ Save The Date ☐ Invitation	
	☐ Yes ☐ No	☐ Save The Date ☐ Invitation	

Guest List

Name	RSVP	Mailed?	Table#
	☐ Yes ☐ No	☐ Save The Date ☐ Invitation	
	☐ Yes ☐ No	☐ Save The Date ☐ Invitation	
	☐ Yes ☐ No	☐ Save The Date ☐ Invitation	
	☐ Yes ☐ No	☐ Save The Date ☐ Invitation	
	☐ Yes ☐ No	☐ Save The Date ☐ Invitation	
	☐ Yes ☐ No	☐ Save The Date ☐ Invitation	
	☐ Yes ☐ No	☐ Save The Date ☐ Invitation	
	☐ Yes ☐ No	☐ Save The Date ☐ Invitation	
	☐ Yes ☐ No	☐ Save The Date ☐ Invitation	
	☐ Yes ☐ No	☐ Save The Date ☐ Invitation	
	☐ Yes ☐ No	☐ Save The Date ☐ Invitation	
	☐ Yes ☐ No	☐ Save The Date ☐ Invitation	

Guest List

Name	RSVP	Mailed?	Table#
	☐ Yes ☐ No	☐ Save The Date ☐ Invitation	
	☐ Yes ☐ No	☐ Save The Date ☐ Invitation	
	☐ Yes ☐ No	☐ Save The Date ☐ Invitation	
	☐ Yes ☐ No	☐ Save The Date ☐ Invitation	
	☐ Yes ☐ No	☐ Save The Date ☐ Invitation	
	☐ Yes ☐ No	☐ Save The Date ☐ Invitation	
	☐ Yes ☐ No	☐ Save The Date ☐ Invitation	
	☐ Yes ☐ No	☐ Save The Date ☐ Invitation	
	☐ Yes ☐ No	☐ Save The Date ☐ Invitation	
	☐ Yes ☐ No	☐ Save The Date ☐ Invitation	
	☐ Yes ☐ No	☐ Save The Date ☐ Invitation	
	☐ Yes ☐ No	☐ Save The Date ☐ Invitation	

Invitations

Name	
Address	

Name	
Address	

Name	
Address	

Name	
Address	

Name	
Address	

Name	
Address	

Invitations

Name	
Address	

Name	
Address	

Name	
Address	

Name	
Address	

Name	
Address	

Name	
Address	

Invitations

Name	
Address	

Name	
Address	

Name	
Address	

Name	
Address	

Name	
Address	

Name	
Address	

Invitations

Name	
Address	

Name	
Address	

Name	
Address	

Name	
Address	

Name	
Address	

Name	
Address	

Invitations

Name	
Address	

Name	
Address	

Name	
Address	

Name	
Address	

Name	
Address	

Name	
Address	

Invitations

Name	
Address	

Name	
Address	

Name	
Address	

Name	
Address	

Name	
Address	

Name	
Address	

Invitations

Name	
Address	

Name	
Address	

Name	
Address	

Name	
Address	

Name	
Address	

Name	
Address	

Invitations

Name	
Address	

Name	
Address	

Name	
Address	

Name	
Address	

Name	
Address	

Name	
Address	

Invitations

Name	
Address	

Name	
Address	

Name	
Address	

Name	
Address	

Name	
Address	

Name	
Address	

Invitations

Name	
Address	

Name	
Address	

Name	
Address	

Name	
Address	

Name	
Address	

Name	
Address	

Seating Planner

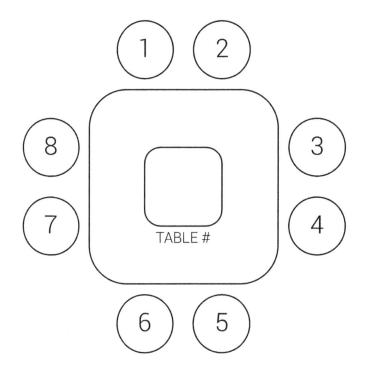

TABLE #

1. _____

2. _____

3. _____

4. _____

5. _____

6. _____

7. _____

8. _____

Seating Planner

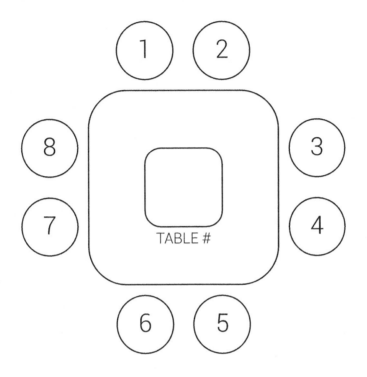

TABLE #

1. _____

2. _____

3. _____

4. _____

5. _____

6. _____

7. _____

8. _____

Seating Planner

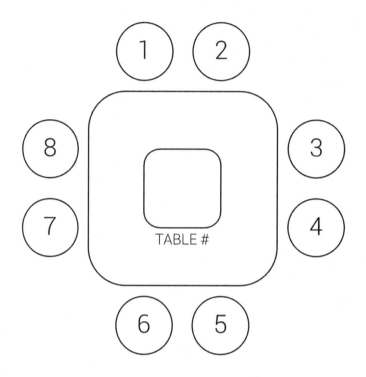

1. _____

2. _____

3. _____

4. _____

5. _____

6. _____

7. _____

8. _____

Seating Planner

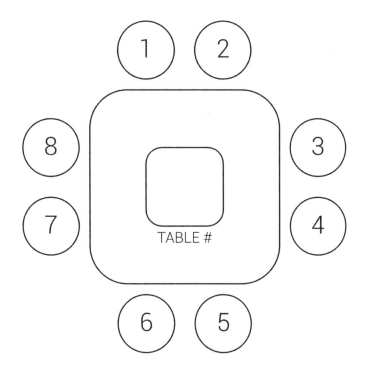

1. _____

2. _____

3. _____

4. _____

5. _____

6. _____

7. _____

8. _____

Seating Planner

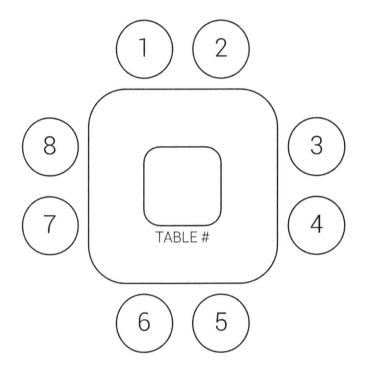

TABLE #

1. _____
2. _____
3. _____
4. _____
5. _____
6. _____
7. _____
8. _____

Seating Planner

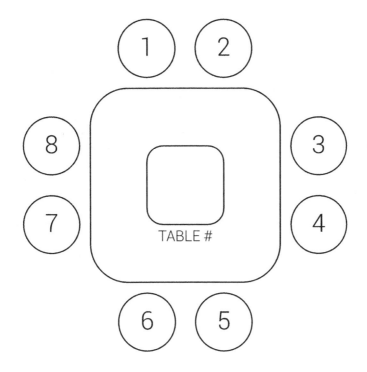

TABLE #

1. _____

2. _____

3. _____

4. _____

5. _____

6. _____

7. _____

8. _____

Seating Planner

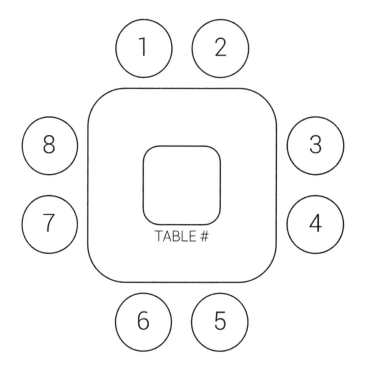

1. _____

2. _____

3. _____

4. _____

5. _____

6. _____

7. _____

8. _____

Seating Planner

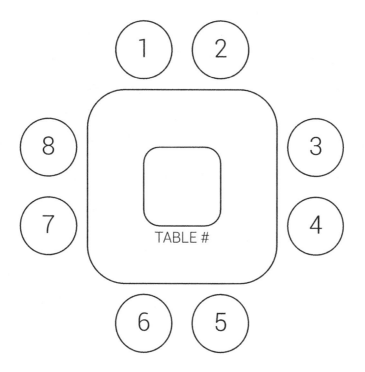

TABLE #

1. _____
2. _____
3. _____
4. _____
5. _____
6. _____
7. _____
8. _____

Seating Planner

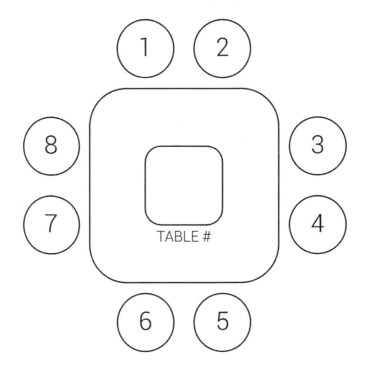

1. _____
2. _____
3. _____
4. _____
5. _____
6. _____
7. _____
8. _____

Seating Planner

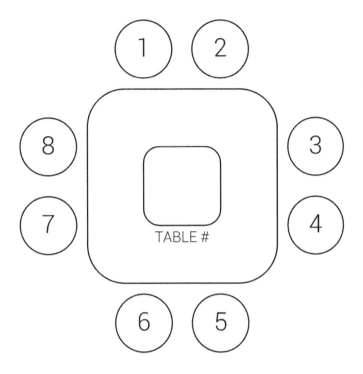

1. _____

2. _____

3. _____

4. _____

5. _____

6. _____

7. _____

8. _____

Seating Planner

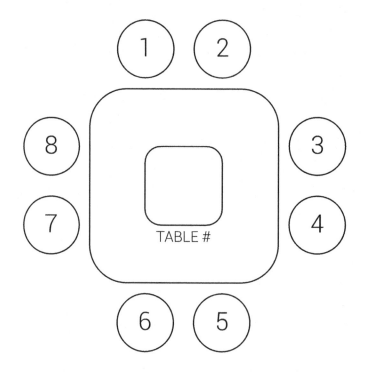

TABLE #

1. _____
2. _____
3. _____
4. _____
5. _____
6. _____
7. _____
8. _____

Seating Planner

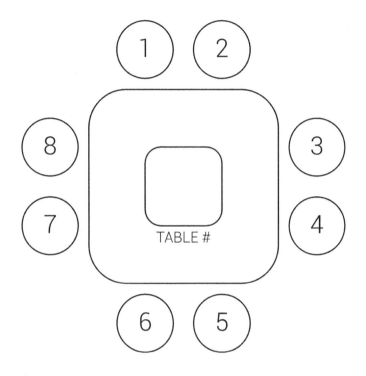

1. _____

2. _____

3. _____

4. _____

5. _____

6. _____

7. _____

8. _____

Seating Planner

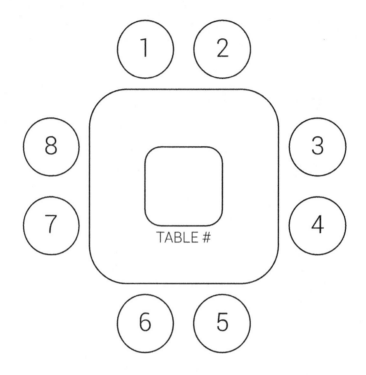

TABLE #

1. _____

2. _____

3. _____

4. _____

5. _____

6. _____

7. _____

8. _____

Seating Planner

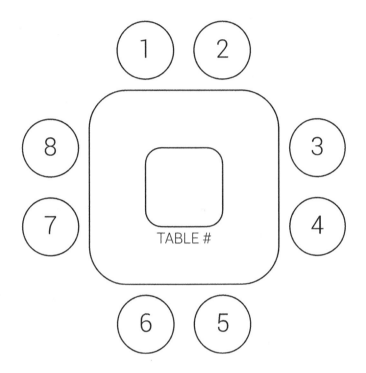

TABLE #

1. _____
2. _____
3. _____
4. _____
5. _____
6. _____
7. _____
8. _____

Seating Planner

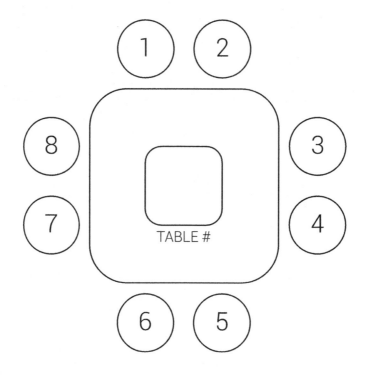

TABLE #

1. _____
2. _____
3. _____
4. _____
5. _____
6. _____
7. _____
8. _____

Seating Planner

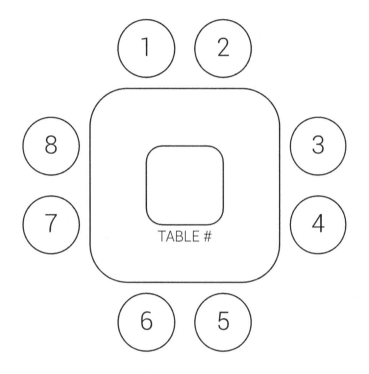

1. _____

2. _____

3. _____

4. _____

5. _____

6. _____

7. _____

8. _____

Notes

Notes

Gifts For Attendance

GIFTS FOR PARENTS OF THE BRIDE & GROOM

Mother of the Bride	
Father of the Bride	
Mother of the Groom	
Father of the Groom	

THE WEDDING PARTY

Maid of Honor	
Bridesmaids	
Best Man	
Groomsmen	
Flowe Girl	
Ring Bearer	
Ushers	
Officiant	

The First Dance

SONG CHOICES

CHOREOGRAPHER

Name	
Phone	
Email	

PRACTICE DATES & TIMES

Our Honeymoon

TRAVEL AGENCY

Name	
Address	
Phone	
Email	
Contact Person	
Notes	

Dates	
Destination	
Legnth of Stay	
Hotel	
Car Rental	

FLIGHT INFORMATION

Departing Flight Number	
Seat Numbers	
Departing Flight Time	
Returning Flight Number	
Seat Numbers	
Returning Flight Time	

For better wedding planning memories view this paper is left blank.

Wedding Planning Memories

_____

_____

_____

_____

_____

_____

_____

_____

_____

_____

_____

_____

_____

_____

_____

_____

_____

_____

_____

_____

_____

_____

_____

_____

_____

_____

Wedding Planning Memories

Wedding Memories

Add your wedding pictures here.

Wedding Memories

Add your wedding pictures here.

Wedding Memories

Add your wedding pictures here.

Wedding Memories

Add your wedding pictures here.

SCAN ME

Made in the USA
Monee, IL
16 February 2022

91270127R00057